Post-Quantum Survival Guide

Defending Data in the Age of Quantum Computing

Jaxon Vale

DEDICATION

This book is dedicated to everyone who is committed to safeguarding the future scientists, researchers, cybersecurity experts, and innovators who put forth endless effort to defend our digital world against impending dangers. We are all inspired by your dedication to expanding knowledge and creating a safer online environment for next generations.

We are grateful to individuals who believe in the power of change, whether they be forward-thinkers, visionaries, or those who embrace the unknown. This is for people who dare to envision a future in which digital security is unwavering in the face of emerging threats and quantum innovations are used for the greater good.

May this work encourage further innovation, teamwork, and readiness in the face of uncertainty, and may it make a modest contribution to the continuing discussion about our digital future.

DISCLAIMER

This book's content is solely intended for informational and educational purposes. Although every attempt has been taken to guarantee the content's authenticity and dependability, the author and publisher make no guarantees or representations about the content's completeness, dependability, or fitness for any particular purpose.

This book is not meant to be a source of professional, financial, or legal advice. Before making judgments based on the information provided, the reader is advised to seek advice from qualified experts, such as cybersecurity specialists, legal counsel, or other pertinent specialists.

The publisher and author disclaim all responsibility for any harm, loss, or damage that results from using or relying on the information in this book, whether directly or indirectly. The author and publisher reserve the right to update and alter the information as needed, and it is subject to change.

All product names, company names, and trademarks mentioned belong to their respective owners.

CONTENTS

ACKNOWLEDGMENTS

This book would not have been possible without the help and efforts of many individuals who have offered their expertise, time, and encouragement during this journey.

First and foremost, I want to sincerely thank my family and friends for their everlasting belief in and support of my work. Their encouragement, understanding, and patience have been a continual source of support.

We would especially want to thank the thought leaders and specialists in the fields of quantum computing and cybersecurity. This book is based on your research, insights, and groundbreaking work in quantum-safe technologies and post-quantum cryptography. Your invaluable contributions to the field have greatly influenced the content and direction of these pages.

Additionally, I want to express my sincere gratitude to the mentors, colleagues, and experts who took the time to offer helpful criticism and comments on the paper. Your advice made it easier to polish the material and guarantee that the book provides accurate and significant insights.

Your ceaseless efforts to safeguard cybersecurity's future have served as an inspiration to the research teams and organizations committed to the development of quantum-safe technologies. It is a privilege for me to add to this significant discussion.

Lastly, I want to express my gratitude to the readers for their interest in this book. I sincerely hope you find the information useful and that it aids in your navigation of the fascinating and always changing fields of post-quantum cryptography and cybersecurity in the future.

I appreciate everyone's participation in this adventure.

CHAPTER 1

THE QUANTUM THREAT: THE NEED FOR CHANGE

1.1 Classical Cryptography's Inadequacy

Our digital world has been safely built upon the foundation of traditional cryptography techniques for many years. From private emails and financial transactions to state secrets and business plans, these systems—like RSA, Elliptic Curve Cryptography (ECC), and symmetric key encryption algorithms—have protected everything. Their success stems from mathematics, notably the tremendous difficulty of solving some mathematical problems with traditional computers, rather than secrecy. However, this once-unshakeable underpinning is starting to crumble as quantum computing advances from theoretical curiosity to emerging reality.

RSA and the Factoring Issue

The mathematical problem of factoring big integers is the

foundation of RSA, one of the most traditional and popular encryption schemes. To put it simply, the outcome of multiplying two very large prime numbers is a number that is incredibly challenging for traditional computers to decipher. This "difficulty gap"—multiplying is simple, while factoring is extremely challenging—is the sole basis for RSA's security.

It could take a traditional supercomputer thousands of years to crack a 2048-bit RSA key. This presumption, however, is only valid in the context of traditional computing. That period could be reduced to a few hours or perhaps minutes due to the development of quantum computers.

The Elliptic Curve Dilemma and ECC

Many people consider Elliptic Curve Cryptography to be RSA's more effective relative. Comparable security levels are attained by ECC with significantly shorter keys and less computing load. It is frequently utilized in blockchain technology, SSL certificates, and mobile devices.

The Elliptic Curve Discrete Logarithm Problem (ECDLP), another issue thought to be impossible for classical machines to solve, is the foundation of ECC's security. However, ECC is susceptible to quantum innovations, much like RSA. ECC can be quickly broken down by algorithms made for quantum computers, especially Shor's Algorithm, making it ineffective for protecting private information.

Symmetric Encryption Is Not Completely Secure

While symmetric algorithms such as AES (Advanced Encryption Standard) are not entirely destroyed by quantum pressure, they are not immune either. A quantum computer can do brute-force key searches in the square root of the time required by a classical computer thanks to Grover's Algorithm.

In the event of a quantum opponent, for instance, the security level provided by AES-128 (with a 128-bit key) may theoretically be cut in half to the equivalent of a 64-bit key. Although raising key sizes (to AES-256, for example) helps lessen this, it's only a short-term, partial fix.

Synopsis

In summary, the durability of classical cryptography is predicated on the existing computational constraints of classical systems rather than on infallible principles. The defenses of contemporary cryptographic systems are being put to the ultimate test as quantum technology redefines their boundaries. It's not a matter of whether but when the regulations will change.

1.2 Quantum Computing's Development

The quantum computer is a completely new paradigm, not just a quicker variant of the classical computer. It does not perform calculations in the same manner as conventional computers. It employs quantum bits or qubits, which are capable of existing in several states concurrently, in place of binary bits. Quantum computers can process large datasets in parallel and explore several solutions simultaneously thanks to a concept known as superposition.

Essential Quantum Ideas That Are Important

It's critical to comprehend a few fundamental ideas in order to comprehend why encryption is at risk from quantum computing:

- One of the classical bits is either 0 or 1. A qubit can simultaneously be either 0 or 1. This makes it possible for quantum systems to investigate many options at once.

- Entanglement: Regardless of the distance between two qubits, the state of one can instantly affect the state of another when they get entangled. Strong quantum operations that are not feasible in classical systems are made possible by this interconnection.

- Quantum Interference: Unlike conventional brute-force methods, quantum computers can use interference to amplify correct channels and cancel out incorrect ones, directing computational effort more effectively.

When applied, these ideas serve as the foundation for a machine that can perform tasks that were previously believed to be computationally impossible.

Shor's Algorithm: The Nightmare of Cryptographers

Shor's Algorithm, created by Peter Shor in 1994, is exponentially quicker than the most well-known classical techniques at factoring large integers. This is disastrous when it comes to cryptography.

Both the discrete logarithm problem (threatening ECC) and the integer factorization problem (threatening RSA) can be effectively resolved by Shor's Algorithm. Essentially, once a sufficiently powerful quantum computer is constructed, the two main public-key cryptography methods currently in use might be completely replaced.

A Hit to Symmetric Keys using Grover's Algorithm

Unlike Shor's algorithm with RSA and ECC, Grover's algorithm weakens symmetric cryptography but does not completely destroy it. It can cut symmetric keys' effective security in half. Double key lengths can counteract this, but it still highlights a fundamental change in threat modeling.

From Concept to Implementation

Quantum computation, which initially appeared to be an intellectual exercise, is now the subject of significant commercial, governmental, and academic interest. National labs, entrepreneurs, and IT behemoths are vying for supremacy in quantum technology. The ramifications for cryptography are now immediate, tangible, and developing quickly rather than being hypothetical.

1.3 Schedules and Actual Threat Situations

A prevalent misunderstanding is that there isn't an immediate threat because quantum computers aren't yet strong enough to decipher contemporary encryption. This way of thinking is dangerously naive.

Forecasts and Developments

The world is already in the midst of a quantum race.

China's National University of Defense Technology, IBM, and Google have all made quantifiable progress in creating practical quantum machines. Despite differing opinions, researchers from the National Institute of Standards and Technology (NIST) in the United States and other authorities predict that practical quantum computers that can crack RSA-2048 will be available in 10 to 20 years, if not sooner.

This timeline is relevant for the following reasons:

- Cryptographic system migration takes years, as legacy data and infrastructure change slowly.
- For decades, sensitive data must be kept safe.

As a result, it would be disastrous to wait for the "quantum moment" to act.

Threats Particular to a Sector

Quantum computing poses hazards in a variety of areas:

- National Security: Adversaries may decrypt military

and intelligence communications that are encrypted today, revealing personnel, assets, and strategy.

- Financial Systems: To ensure safe transactions, banks, trading platforms, and central institutions mainly rely on encryption. Whole economies could become unstable due to a leak.

- Healthcare and Personal Data: To protect privacy, genomic information, personal identifiers, and medical records are all encrypted. Public access to historical and current records would be possible through quantum decryption.

- Critical Infrastructure: Networked, encrypted systems are becoming more and more important for water supply, power grids, and air traffic control systems. Chaos in the actual world could result from a successful breach.

The unsettling truth is that several of these industries already have to contend with highly skilled competitors, many of whom are getting ready for a quantum advantage in the future.

1.4 The "Harvest Now, Decrypt Later" concept.

What is quietly harvested for future decryption, rather than what can be decrypted today, may be the most subtly serious threat in the quantum age.

How It Operates

Even if they are currently unable to decrypt encrypted data, many cyber adversaries, state actors in particular, are already intercepting and storing encrypted data. The concept is straightforward:

- As much encrypted traffic as you can from certain sources, including as emails, financial records, VPN streams, and secret communications, should be intercepted now.

- Store for the future: These datasets will be unreadable for now so securely archive them.

- Decrypt when ready: Use Shor's or Grover's technique to break the encryption and retrieve the data once quantum computers have the necessary processing power.

The Harvest Now, Decrypt Later (HNDL) technique takes advantage of the gap between data transfer and the obsolescence of cryptography. The clock is ticking.

Why It's Important Now

Even while there aren't any dangerously large quantum computers yet, the data that is taken now could be compromised later. Consider:

- Decades-important diplomatic cables
- Business trade secrets pertaining to financial projections, product design, or intellectual property
- Long-term military plans or intelligence dossiers
- Personal information that could be used in future identity theft

The HNDL threat is particularly serious because of the

temporal discrepancy between encryption lifespans and data sensitivity.

Countering the Danger

To counter this threat, immediate, aggressive changes are needed:

- Sensitive systems should begin moving to post-quantum cryptography algorithms.
- Revise data governance guidelines to consider encrypted data that has been encrypted for a long time as possibly vulnerable.
- Inform interested parties on the long-term nature of risk and digital secrecy.

The quantum threat is today's strategic imperative it is not tomorrow's problem. The security of traditional cryptography techniques is no longer assured in the years to come. A fundamental change in our understanding, application, and defense of digital security is brought about by quantum computing. It is no longer safe to wait. Both the digital and quantum clocks are running out of time

CHAPTER 2

FOUNDATIONS AND CAPABILITIES OF QUANTUM COMPUTING

As ground-breaking discoveries from the once theoretical field of quantum physics emerge, the world is experiencing a technological revolution. Long considered a fringe idea, quantum computing is quickly developing into a revolutionary force with wide-ranging effects. Its capabilities go beyond what is possible with traditional computing, ranging from materials science and cryptography to artificial intelligence and optimization. We must first comprehend the fundamental ideas and technical difficulties of quantum computing in order to appreciate how it affects existing encryption techniques and how it promises previously unheard-of processing capability.

2.1 Superposition and Quantum Bits

The distinctions between qubits and classical bits

The fundamental unit of information sits at the heart of every computer, whether it is a classical or quantum machine. Bits are used to represent data in classical computing, and they can be either 0 or 1. In classical systems, these binary digits serve as the fundamental units of all operations.

In contrast, quantum bits or qubits are used in quantum computing. In contrast to classical bits, qubits can exist concurrently in a combination of 0 and 1 since they are controlled by the laws of quantum mechanics. Superposition is the name given to this attribute.

To picture this idea:

- Comparable to a light switch, a classical bit can be either ON (1) or OFF (0).
- A point on the Bloch sphere's surface represents the state of a qubit, which functions similarly to a dimmer switch attached to a sphere. It can exist in any linear combination (superposition) of the pure 0 and pure 1 states.

For some kinds of problems, like factoring big numbers or mimicking quantum systems, the capability of quantum computers increases exponentially due to their special capacity to process many states simultaneously.

An Overview of Quantum Entanglement

Entanglement is another characteristic that distinguishes quantum mechanics and, thus, quantum computing. This phenomenon happens when two or more qubits are connected in such a way that, regardless of their distance from one another, the state of one qubit directly influences the state of the other.

Qubits can coordinate their states in ways that are not possible in conventional systems thanks to entanglement. Quantum computers can execute some tasks more quickly than classical machines thanks to this interconnection, which also significantly boosts computing power.

In an entangled system, for instance:

When one qubit is measured, its entangled partner's state is instantly revealed. Multiple entangled qubit computations allow for the simultaneous exploration of a large solution space, opening the door to algorithms that are not possible on traditional hardware.

Quantum speedup, the phenomenon wherein quantum computers solve problems significantly quicker than their classical counterparts, is made possible by superposition and entanglement working together.

2.2 Circuits and Gates in Quantum

How Circuits Are Made and How Quantum Gates Work

Quantum computers use quantum gates to control qubits, just as conventional computers use logic gates (AND, OR, NOT) to carry out operations. But in order to maintain quantum coherence, quantum gates need unitary transformations to work with the probabilities and phases of qubit states.

Quantum gates are capable of:

- Rotate the state of a qubit (such as an X, Y, or Z gate) on the Bloch sphere.
- Put a qubit into superposition using a Hadamard gate, for example.
- Entanglement between qubits is introduced (e.g., CNOT gate).
- Utilize qubit-state-based conditional logic.

These gates are connected in sequence to create quantum circuits. Quantum information flows via these circuits in a fundamentally different way than classical logic, frequently depending on probabilistic results and interference patterns.

Typical quantum circuits could:

- Set up qubits in a certain superposition at first. Use entangling gates to establish correlations.
- Adjust phase amplitudes to make accurate responses stand out.
- To determine the outcome, measure the end state.

All quantum algorithms rely on these circuits, whose design must take into consideration issues unique to quantum computing, such as coherence and reversibility.

Challenges with Measurement and Decoherence

The sensitivity of quantum systems is quite high. Decoherence the loss of quantum behavior as a result of interaction with the environment is one of the most difficult problems in the construction and upkeep of quantum computers.

Measurement is yet another important issue. When a quantum state is measured, it collapses into a classical state. This implies:

- The superposition is destroyed
- Only one of the possible outcomes is observed
- All other information recorded in the qubit's quantum state is lost

Because of this vulnerability, quantum programming is very different. Circuit designers must minimize the damaging impacts of measurement and ambient noise while creating circuits that extract valuable information.

Fault-tolerant architectures and quantum error correction algorithms are being actively researched to address these problems, but they are quite sophisticated and resource-intensive.

2.3 Prominent Algorithms in Quantum

Shor's Factoring Algorithm

Peter Shor's introduction of a quantum algorithm in 1994 rocked the cryptography establishment. In a reasonable amount of time, Shor's algorithm effectively factors huge integers, something that traditional algorithms find difficult to accomplish.

The importance?

- One of the most used encryption techniques, RSA encryption, depends on how hard it is to factor big integers.

- This task's sub-exponential (best classical) time complexity can be reduced to polynomial time using Shor's technique.
- The development of sufficiently big quantum computers may make RSA encryption obsolete.

In short, this is how it operates:

- To determine the period of a modular function, Shor's technique employs a quantum subroutine known as the Quantum Fourier Transform (QFT). This time frame makes it possible to pinpoint the goal number's contributing causes.
- In order to identify patterns that are not visible to classical processors, the entire procedure depends on quantum parallelism and interference.

Search Algorithm by Groover

For unstructured search tasks, Grover's algorithm offers a notable quantum speedup, albeit not as devastating as Shor's for cryptographic systems.

In systems that are classical:

- It takes $O(N)$ time to search an unsorted database with N entries.
- This is reduced to $O(\sqrt{N})$, a quadratic improvement, by Grover's technique.

Among the applications are:

- Accelerating brute-force attacks against symmetric encryption, such as AES
- Optimizing intricate search issues in decision science, logistics, and artificial intelligence

Modern cryptography recommendations are influenced by the fact that, while quantum computers that run Grover's method wouldn't totally crack symmetric encryption, they would need to double key sizes to retain similar security.

2.4 Scalability and Quantum Hardware

An Overview of Photonic, Ion-Trap, and Superconducting Quantum Computers

Not only is quantum computing theoretical, but it is also being developed on a variety of hardware platforms, each with its own advantages and disadvantages.

1. Superconducting Qubits (like those made by Google and IBM):

Use Josephson junctions, which act like artificial atoms; cool to almost zero to reduce noise and decoherence; operate quickly; have strong commercial support; and are currently at the forefront of development infrastructure and qubit count.

2. Ion-Trap Qubits (like Honeywell's IonQ):

Qubits are encoded in the atomic energy levels; they are used to represent individual charged atoms caught in electromagnetic fields.

- Exceptionally high coherence and fidelity times
- Reduced gate speeds yet extremely precise operations

3. Photonic qubits, such as PsiQuantum and Xanadu:

Encode data in photon characteristics, such as polarization.

- Naturally resistant to decoherence because of minimal environmental interaction; capable of room temperature operation and simple fiber optic connection; yet in the early phases of circuit-level manipulation

Every kind of hardware signifies a distinct route to achieving the potential of quantum computing. But there are trade-offs for each, and there isn't yet a clear "winner."

Difficulties in Quantum System Scaling

Scaling quantum systems from tens to millions of qubits is still extremely difficult, even with recent advancements. Important obstacles include:

- Due to their susceptibility to noise, quantum gates necessitate error correction.
- Qubits must stay in superposition for the duration of computations, which is known as the "coherence

time."

- Connectivity: It is challenging to coordinate effective multi-qubit interactions at scale.
- Control systems: To handle qubit states, quantum processors require accurate, fast control hardware.

Although necessary, quantum error correction necessitates a great deal of redundancy. To produce a single logical qubit, some approaches need hundreds of physical qubits. This significantly raises the amount of resources needed for realistic quantum computing.

With major advancements anticipated over the next ten years, research institutions and businesses around the world are vying to overcome these challenges. The long-term viability and impact of quantum hardware will ultimately depend on its ability to scale successfully.

A fundamental change in how we perceive and use information is represented by quantum computing. Its foundations are found in the peculiar yet potent ideas of quantum mechanics, which allow systems to handle data in ways that were previously impossible for traditional computers.

We may grasp why quantum computing is not merely a curiosity but an inevitable future by comprehending the subtleties of qubits, the workings of quantum gates and circuits, the revolutionary possibilities of algorithms like Shor's and Grover's, and the enormous efforts to create scalable hardware. One that demands a quick review of the technologies we now use, especially in areas like scientific research, cybersecurity, and optimization.

The quantum era is among us; it is not a far-off fantasy. Preparing for the significant transformation it promises to bring requires first understanding its base

CHAPTER 3

THE RACE TO POST-QUANTUM CRYPTOGRAPHY

3.1 Post-Quantum Cryptography: What Is It?

A hidden but crucial race is taking place in the field of cybersecurity as quantum computing advances faster: the race to protect digital data from quantum assaults. At the forefront of this challenge is Post-Quantum Cryptography (PQC), which is not a futuristic idea but rather a requirement stemming from the flaws in the current cryptographic infrastructure.

PQC Definition and Goals

A collection of cryptographic methods known as "post-quantum cryptography" are made to withstand both classical and quantum computational attacks. Even though modern encryption techniques like RSA and ECC (Elliptic Curve Cryptography) are resistant to assaults from classical computers, sufficiently powerful quantum machines may readily crack them using algorithms like Shor's.

- PQC's primary objective is quantum-resilient security. That is, to keep data storage and transmission viable on existing classical systems while protecting them from the exponential power of quantum computation.

- PQC is wholly software-based in contrast to quantum cryptography, which relies on the physical concepts of quantum physics (e.g., quantum key distribution via photons). In the short term, it is a more accessible and scalable defense mechanism because it can operate on current hardware.

The Differences in Quantum Cryptography

Given the frequent confusion between the terminology, it is imperative to comprehend the differences between Quantum Cryptography and Post-Quantum Cryptography (PQC). Although they both seek to protect data from quantum attacks, their theoretical underpinnings and real-world applications are quite different.

A summary of their distinctions in a number of important areas is provided below:

1. Basis of Foundation:

- Complex mathematical problems that are thought to be difficult for both classical and quantum computers to solve are the foundation of post-quantum cryptography. Lattice-based, code-based, and multivariate polynomial cryptography are a few examples.
- The laws of quantum mechanics, such as superposition and entanglement, are the foundation of Quantum Cryptography, which enables the establishment of secure communication channels that are capable of detecting eavesdropping.

2. Hardware Requirements:

- The methods used in post-quantum cryptography are intended to operate on classical computing infrastructure. They can be implemented using current digital systems and don't require any extra hardware.

- The implementation of quantum cryptography is more complicated and expensive because it requires specialized quantum hardware, such as quantum key distribution (QKD) systems and quantum communication links (such as fiber optics or satellite-based entanglement systems).

3. Model of Security:

- A sufficiently powerful quantum computer could launch assaults like Shor's algorithm, which jeopardizes the security of existing public-key cryptosystems. PQC protects against these threats.

- Quantum Cryptography, particularly QKD, uses the idea that measuring a quantum system invariably upsets it to secure communication by physically detecting any eavesdropping efforts.

4. Preparedness for Deployment:

- Post-Quantum Cryptography is suited for widespread adoption today and is currently being standardized by institutions such as NIST. Numerous algorithms are currently in advanced phases of deployment or evaluation.

- Despite being a promising innovation, quantum cryptography is still in early deployment or research phases. Because of the infrastructure and knowledge needed, it is mostly limited to specialized or extremely secure contexts.

5. Scalability:

- Because it readily fits into current communication protocols, such TLS, VPNs, and email encryption, without requiring significant architectural changes, PQC is highly scalable.

- One drawback of quantum cryptography is its limited scalability. Without substantial expenditure, it is not feasible for worldwide, decentralized use due to the requirement for direct quantum communication connections and reliable relays.

Quantum Cryptography is essentially a radical change to physics-based communication protocols, whereas Post-Quantum Cryptography is mostly about fortifying our current cryptographic systems using new math. Depending on the particular threat model and context, they can be complementary in a layered cybersecurity strategy, but they are not interchangeable solutions.

This is not just an academic distinction. PQC is the workable, internationally applicable solution to the impending quantum menace.

3.2 Domestic and International Reactions

Global cybersecurity agencies and governments are aware of the urgency of PQC. A concerted multinational effort to migrate cryptographic infrastructure in time has been sparked by the expectation of quantum decryption capabilities, also known as "Y2Q" (Years to Quantum).

PQC Standardization Project at NIST

A key player in the formalization of PQC standards is the National Institute of Standards and Technology (NIST) of the United States. NIST established a global open competition in 2016 to find and define new algorithms that can withstand quantum assaults because it realized that the widely used RSA and ECC will become outdated in a quantum environment.

Phases make up the structure of the NIST PQC project:

- Submission and Evaluation: Cryptographers from all around the world submitted more than 80 algorithm proposals.
- Rounds of Reduction: NIST reduced the pool in several rounds by means of performance benchmarking, cryptanalytic testing, and thorough analysis.
- Finalists and Standards: NIST announced four algorithms in 2022: CRYSTALS-Dilithium, FALCON, and SPHINCS+ for digital signatures and CRYSTALS-Kyber for key encapsulation.

The following criteria were used to choose these

algorithms:

- The ability to withstand both classical and quantum attacks
- Efficiency in terms of both software and hardware; robustness and simplicity of implementation

Importantly, standardization is a foundation, not the end of the process. These algorithms must now be incorporated into platforms, devices, and protocols throughout the digital ecosystem by agencies, businesses, and developers.

Participation of International Research and Cybersecurity Agencies

The United States is not alone in its response to the quantum menace. There is growing international agreement regarding the urgency of PQC migration:

- Europe: Proactive research and public-private collaboration have been highlighted by ENISA (European Union Agency for Cybersecurity) and the European Telecommunications Standards Institute

(ETSI).

- Asia-Pacific: To address a variety of threat vectors, nations including Japan, South Korea, and Singapore are investing in both PQC and quantum communication research.

- Australia and Canada: Both countries are actively working on national policies for quantum-resilient infrastructure and are taking part in NIST's process.

In addition to standardization, a significant trend among international agencies is collaborative implementation, the understanding that worldwide interoperability is necessary for secure communications in the quantum era.

3.3 Threat Models and Security Levels

We must comprehend how vulnerabilities are evaluated and the particular kinds of assaults that post-quantum algorithms are designed to fend off in order to appreciate the significance of PQC.

Quantum Resistance Evaluation

Even when known attacks are carried out by quantum computers, PQC algorithms are made to be computationally impossible to crack. This includes opposition to:

- Shor's Algorithm: Effectively factoring huge integers and computing discrete logarithms, this algorithm can break RSA, DSA, and ECC.
- Grover's Algorithm: Lowers the security margin of symmetric algorithms (like AES) without sacrificing their efficacy by providing a quadratic speedup for brute-force attacks.

Therefore, asymmetric cryptosystems (public-key encryption, digital signatures) need to be totally replaced, even though symmetric algorithms merely need longer keys to stay secure.

PQC security levels are assessed using security bits that are comparable to traditional cryptography standards:

- Level 1: AES-128 security equivalent;
- Level 3: AES-192 security equivalent;

- Level 5: AES-256 security equivalent

These levels give suppliers and developers a starting point for choosing the best performance-security trade-off.

Different Attack Types

When evaluating PQC readiness, a number of attack classes are pertinent:

- The term "Quantum-Specific Attacks" refers to algorithms, like the ones described above, that take advantage of quantum capabilities.
- Classical Attacks: Implementation-specific vulnerabilities and side-channel vulnerabilities remain relevant.
- Hybrid Attacks: Incorporate both classical and quantum components, perhaps combining machine learning and brute-force techniques to compromise less resilient post-quantum systems.
- Physical leaks like as timing, power usage, or electromagnetic emissions can be exploited in Side-Channel Attacks. Whatever the algorithmic

strength, PQC implementations need to be reinforced against these.

Security is operational as well as mathematical. Implementations need to be stable at both the hardware and software levels.

3.4 Evaluation Standards for PQC Algorithms

A wide range of technical and practical indicators are needed to evaluate PQC candidates, as there are dozens of suggested methods.

Flexibility, Performance, Key Size, and Efficiency

Adoption is driven by practical usage, even when theoretical security is crucial. Important evaluation standards consist of:

- PQC algorithms typically have larger key sizes than RSA or ECC, which might have an impact on storage, memory, and network bandwidth. For instance:

- RSA-2048: just about 256 bytes
- Kyber-1024: Ciphertext ~1.6 KB; public key ~1.5 KB
- Computational Performance: Algorithms need to function well on high-performance servers and low-power Internet of Things devices. Dilithium and CRYSTALS-Kyber have proven to perform quickly on several platforms.
- Signature and Ciphertext Sizes: Particularly important in settings where bandwidth is limited, such as mobile networks and embedded systems.
- Flexibility: For a variety of applications and future-proofing, algorithms that provide numerous security levels or parameter sets are favored.

Readiness for Migration and Interoperability

The key question in PQC adoption is how smoothly migration can happen, not if it will. Migration preparedness takes into account:

- Hybrid Cryptography: To facilitate the transition and guarantee backward compatibility, some organizations are implementing hybrid schemes that combine PQC and classical algorithms.

- PQC algorithms must be able to be readily included into current protocols, such as TLS, SSH, and VPNs, without necessitating significant changes.

- Simplicity of Implementation: Codebases that are readable, maintainable, and verifiable improve trust and lower integration errors.

- The adoption of algorithms that are royalty-free and open-source is accelerated, especially by public-sector organizations and open-standard consortia.

Upgrading cryptographic systems without interfering with services is an impending challenge for governments, financial organizations, cloud providers, and healthcare networks. Algorithms must be *adoptable* in addition to being robust.

Post-quantum cryptography is a modern necessity, not a problem for the future. The systems safeguarding routine communications, national security, and digital commerce are under jeopardy as quantum computing gets closer to being useful.

It is a technological and organizational marathon to get to PQC. Governments, businesses, developers, and end users are all involved in addition to cryptographers. PQC provides a road map for a safe digital environment that is robust no matter what the future of computation brings thanks to international collaboration, progressive standards, and flexible implementations

CHAPTER 4

LEADING POST-QUANTUM ALGORITHMS AND STANDARDS

Making sure that the security methods in use today can survive the processing capability of future quantum computers is one of the main concerns facing cryptography as the era of quantum computing approaches. A crucial field of research is post-quantum cryptography (PQC), which aims to create cryptographic algorithms that are immune to quantum attacks. The most promising post-quantum algorithms are examined in this chapter along with the fundamental ideas that underpin their resilience to quantum computing and how they relate to the broader context of contemporary cryptography requirements.

4.1 Cryptography Based on Code

One of the earliest and most studied post-quantum cryptography techniques is code-based cryptography. It is based on mathematical constructs called error-correcting codes, which are intended to identify and fix transmission faults. These codes are a promising option for upcoming cryptographic systems since they are naturally immune to quantum attacks.

Synopsis of Classic McEliece Algorithms

Classic McEliece is the most famous example of code-based cryptography. This approach, which was first proposed by Robert McEliece in 1978, makes use of the Goppa codes family of error-correcting codes. The security of the classic McEliece public-key encryption system is dependent on the difficulty of decoding a random linear code, which is still a computationally challenging task even for quantum computers.

Two keys are used by Classic McEliece to operate:

- Public Key: Contains a matrix that enables message encryption and details about the construction of the code.
- To decode messages encrypted using the public key,

use the Private Key.

Since the fundamental decoding problem is thought to be challenging for quantum computers, as opposed to issues like integer factorization and discrete logarithms, which are susceptible to Shor's method, the primary benefit of this cryptosystem is its resistance to quantum attacks.

Advantages and Drawbacks

Advantages:

- Quantum Resistance: The Classic McEliece algorithm is a formidable competitor in the battle for quantum-resistant cryptography since it is thought to be safe against both classical and quantum computers.

- Mature Research: There is a great degree of confidence in the security of code-based cryptography because it has been thoroughly investigated throughout the years, and Classic McEliece in particular.

- Efficient Decoding: Although the encryption procedure requires a lot of computing power, the decryption step (using the private key) is comparatively quick, which is a big plus for real-world applications.

Restrictions:

- huge Key Sizes: The huge key sizes required for code-based cryptography are one of its main disadvantages. Classic McEliece public keys can be hundreds of kilobytes in size, which can cause issues with performance, transmission, and storage.
- Implementation Complexity: Compared to other cryptographic techniques, Classic McEliece's error-correcting codes can be more difficult to implement due to their mathematical complexity.

Classic McEliece's strong theoretical underpinnings and quantum resistance make it one of the top candidates for post-quantum encryption, notwithstanding its drawbacks.

4.2 Cryptography Based on Lattices

A class of cryptographic techniques known as "lattice-based cryptography" is predicated on how difficult problems involving geometric lattices in multi-dimensional environments are. Lattice-based techniques are a possible option for post-quantum cryptography since these issues are thought to be challenging even for quantum computers.

Algorithms such as Falcon, Dilithium, and Kyber

The well-known lattice-based algorithms Kyber, Dilithium, and Falcon are among those under consideration for standardization.

A key encapsulation method (KEM) for safe key exchange is called Kyber. It relies on the hardness of the Learning With Errors (LWE) problem, a core problem in lattice-based cryptography. Kyber is a popular option for post-quantum key exchange since it has been demonstrated to be effective and safe.

Another digital signature system that uses lattice problems is called Dilithium. The Ring-Learning With Errors (Ring-LWE) problem, a variation of LWE that maximizes lattice structure to improve the efficiency of cryptographic operations, serves as its foundation. In a world where quantum security is guaranteed, dilithium is a promising option for digital signatures since it provides great security with moderate key sizes.

Falcon is another lattice-based digital signature system that uses ring-based lattice structures and is based on the NTRU problem. It is an excellent fit for applications that need both security and performance because it offers small signatures and is made to be effective even in low-resource contexts.

The Resistance of Lattices to Quantum Attacks

Lattice-based cryptography relies on the challenge of resolving issues like:

- The task of solving a system of noisy linear equations is known as "Learning With Errors (LWE)" and is thought to be challenging for both classical and quantum computers.
- Finding the smallest non-zero vector in a lattice is the aim of the smallest Vector Problem (SVP), which is a computationally challenging task even for

quantum computers.

- Finding the vector that is nearest to a specific point in a lattice is known as the "Closest Vector Problem" (CVP), and it is regarded as a challenging task for quantum algorithms.

Lattice-based cryptography is one of the most promising options for post-quantum security because, while quantum computers may have exponential speedups for discrete logarithms and integer factorization, they are unable to solve lattice problems like LWE and SVP. This is because quantum algorithms, such as Shor's algorithm, cannot solve these problems.

Advantages:

- Efficient Performance: Lattice-based algorithms, especially Kyber and Dilithium, are renowned for their effectiveness, which makes them appropriate for devices with limited resources as well as large-scale systems.
- Scalability: As security levels rise, lattice-based systems can scale more readily, providing quick operations and appropriate key sizes.

Restrictions:

- Key and Signature Sizes: Lattice-based systems still need bigger key and signature sizes than classical schemes, despite being more compact than code-based systems. Nevertheless, advancements in this area are ongoing.

- The implementation of lattice-based algorithms is difficult and necessitates certain mathematical knowledge.

4.3 Hash-Based and Multivariate Signatures

While post-quantum encryption is dominated by code-based and lattice-based cryptographic techniques, multivariate and hash-based signature schemes provide an alternate strategy that is becoming more popular due to its effectiveness and resilience.

Algorithms like SPHINCS+ and Rainbow

- Rainbow: Drawing on the challenge of solving systems of multivariate quadratic equations over finite fields, Rainbow is a digital signature scheme based on multivariate quadratic equations. Rainbow is a promising option for safe digital signatures since these issues are thought to be challenging even for quantum computers.

- SPHINCS+: SPHINCS+ is a hash-based signature technique that generates digital signatures by utilizing the security of hash functions. It is immune to quantum attacks since it does not depend on conventional number-theoretic issues like discrete logarithm problem or integer factorization. SPHINCS+ and other hash-based signatures can provide robust security with comparatively easy and effective implementations.

Performance Metrics and Use Cases

- Rainbow: Rainbow is especially helpful when quick signature generation and small key sizes are essential. In contrast to lattice-based methods, it has bigger public key sizes, which could restrict its application in settings where key size is crucial.

- SPHINCS+: With hash functions that have undergone extensive testing over time, SPHINCS+ is perfect for settings that demand high security. Although it performs competitively, some use cases, such as IoT devices or systems with strict bandwidth limits, may be impacted by its signature sizes, which can be bigger than those of other post-quantum alternatives.

Advantages:

- Rainbow: Offers quick signature verification and comparatively tiny signatures, which is crucial in applications that require quick turnaround times.
- SPHINCS+: Makes use of proven cryptographic primitives (hash functions) that are extremely effective and resistant to quantum errors.

Drawbacks:

- Rainbow: Potential bottlenecks in key creation and large public key sizes.
- SPHINCS+: Although the algorithm is safe, its wider use in bandwidth-constrained settings may be

hampered by the size of its signatures in comparison to other post-quantum techniques.

4.4 Key Encapsulation Mechanisms vs Digital Signatures

Knowing the difference between digital signatures and key encapsulation mechanisms (KEMs) is crucial in post-quantum cryptography. Although they are both basic cryptographic primitives, their functions and implementations in post-quantum systems differ.

Recognizing Various Cryptographic Positions

- Digital Signatures: These are used to verify the sender's identity and guarantee the message's integrity. They offer a means of confirming that a communication hasn't been tampered with while being transmitted. Digital signatures that are immune to quantum errors are provided by post-quantum cryptography techniques such as Dilithium and Falcon.

- KEMs, or key encapsulation mechanisms, are: These are employed in secure key exchange, which allows two people to safely create a shared secret key via an unprotected channel of communication. One well-known example of a quantum-resistant KEM that is well respected for safe key exchange is the Kyber method.

PQC Methods for Encryption and Signatures

- Signatures in PQC: Post-quantum digital signatures that are impervious to quantum attacks are offered by algorithms like Dilithium, Falcon, and SPHINCS+. In a quantum-secure setting, these signatures aid in guaranteeing the legitimacy of communications.

- Algorithms such as Kyber and NTRU provide secure key establishment for key exchange, wherein the shared keys are packaged and subsequently extracted by both parties for encryption and decryption applications.

Important Distinctions: Digital signatures confirm the legitimacy and

- data integrity.
- Cryptographic keys can be securely exchanged thanks to KEMs.

Both digital signatures and KEMs are essential components of a comprehensive post-quantum cryptography system, which guarantees data integrity and safe communication in the quantum era.

Post-quantum cryptography is a broad area that encompasses a variety of techniques and algorithms aimed at addressing the looming quantum threat to traditional cryptographic systems. Code-based, lattice-based, multivariate, and hash-based cryptography are the methods discussed in this chapter, and each has unique advantages and disadvantages. The future of secure communication in a quantum world will rely on a careful selection and combination of these approaches as we continue to improve them and strive for standardization, guaranteeing security and performance across a range of applications

CHAPTER 5

MIGRATION TECHNIQUES–MAKING THE SWITCH TO POST-QUANTUM CRYPTOGRAPHY (PQC)

Organizations that depend on encryption to protect sensitive data face a significant problem as quantum computing develops and has the potential to upend established cryptographic solutions. The transition to post-quantum cryptography (PQC) is a planned, lengthy process that requires careful management rather than a sudden, one-time change. This chapter will examine PQC migration options, including evaluating the quantum risk of current infrastructure, putting hybrid systems into place, and overcoming any obstacles.

5.1 Evaluating Current Infrastructure's Quantum Risk

Organizations must have a thorough understanding of the quantum dangers that could jeopardize their current cryptographic systems before starting the process of switching to PQC. To guarantee a seamless and successful transition to quantum-resistant technologies, a thorough evaluation of the existing infrastructure is required.

Cryptographic Asset Inventory

Performing a comprehensive inventory of all cryptographic assets in use throughout the company is the first step in evaluating quantum risk. This entails determining whose digital signatures, encryption methods, key exchange protocols, and authentication techniques are presently in use in both legacy and production systems.

- Systems for Public Key Infrastructure (PKI): These systems might employ quantum-attack-prone algorithms like RSA, ECDSA, or DH (Diffie-Hellman). It is essential to determine which components of the infrastructure rely on these algorithms.

- Protocols for Data Storage and Communication: Think about the ways that private information is communicated (e.g., HTTPS, VPNs) and stored (e.g., encrypted databases). Quantum computers have the potential to compromise any encryption techniques used to protect this data.

- Third-Party Dependencies: Examine any libraries, services, or cryptographic tools that are part of your systems; they might also use techniques that are susceptible to quantum attacks.

Following the mapping of the cryptographic landscape, businesses can evaluate the possible threats that quantum computers may pose. The necessity of switching to PQC becomes evident if the current infrastructure mainly uses classical algorithms that are susceptible to quantum attacks.

Evaluations of Quantum Readiness

An organization's level of preparedness for implementing PQC and safeguarding its systems against potential quantum threats can be ascertained through a quantum readiness assessment. Usually, this evaluation consists of:

- Risk Assessment: How important are cryptographic resources? What might happen if there is a breach or if quantum attackers decipher it? High-risk assets, such financial or personal data, need to be handled more quickly.

- Quantum Threat Timeline: Although the exact time frame for the development of large-scale quantum computers is yet unknown, projections indicate that quantum capabilities would be adequate to crack existing cryptography schemes within the next ten to twenty years. Prioritizing migration activities will be made easier by evaluating this timeline.

- Analysis of Vulnerabilities: To what extent are your current cryptographic solutions robust? Can the existing systems be improved, or would a total redesign be required?

- Cost-Benefit Consideration: Time, money, and resources may be expended throughout the PQC transition. It's critical to weigh the dangers of quantum vulnerabilities against the possible expenses of updating to systems that are immune to quantum errors.

Organizations can better understand the extent of the required migration and the urgency of switching to PQC solutions by carrying out these studies.

5.2 Systems of Hybrid Cryptography

The use of hybrid cryptography systems is among the best methods for making the switch to PQC. These technologies enable businesses to progressively adopt PQC without totally stopping their operations by combining classical (quantum-vulnerable) and post-quantum (quantum-resistant) algorithms in a staggered fashion.

Integrating PQC and Classical for a Phased Approach

During the transition phase, hybrid cryptography systems are made to take advantage of the advantages of both conventional and quantum-resistant algorithms. An organization might, for instance, implement a hybrid encryption scheme in which post-quantum algorithms are also utilized to secure new communications and systems, while classical encryption algorithms are used for instant compatibility. This guarantees that systems are safe from present and potential threats while facilitating a seamless migration path.

- Key Exchange: A hybrid approach to key exchange may combine quantum-resistant techniques like Kyber (a lattice-based KEM) with conventional techniques like Diffie-Hellman. This two-pronged strategy guarantees that future attackers with quantum capabilities won't be able to take advantage of traditional weaknesses.

- Digital Signatures: In a similar vein, hybrid digital signatures can be used, which combine post-quantum alternatives like Dilithium or Falcon with conventional signatures like RSA or ECDSA. By doing this, businesses make sure that the signature is secure even in the event that an adversary uses quantum capabilities.

Organizations can gradually phase out the classical

components and make the whole switch to quantum-resistant systems as PQC algorithms gain traction and are demonstrated.

Benefits, Drawbacks, and Implementation Techniques

Advantages:

- Smooth Transition: By allowing for a more gradual migration, hybrid systems lower the risks associated with implementing a brand-new system all at once.
- Hybrid systems guarantee backward compatibility with third-party services and legacy systems that might not yet support PQC.
- Decreased Risk: The overall security is more resilient throughout the transition phase, offering dual protection, because both classical and post-quantum techniques are employed.

Drawbacks:

- Increased Complexity: Compared to using a single cryptographic technique, deploying and maintaining a hybrid system is more complicated. Both classical and quantum-resistant systems require careful management, which may present operational difficulties.

- Performance Overhead: Because both classical and quantum-resistant algorithms require extra computations, there may be some performance overhead.

- Long-Term Transition: Organizations will eventually need to make the complete switch to PQC in order to guarantee long-term security, as hybrid systems may not provide the same level of security as fully post-quantum solutions.

Deployment Strategies:

- Pilot Projects: Prior to implementing PQC algorithms throughout the entire company, begin with pilot projects to test their integration in a controlled setting.

- The hybrid system should be implemented in phases, starting with the most important systems and working your way up as trust in PQC increases.

- Monitoring and Evaluation: Keep an eye on the hybrid system's security and performance to make sure it satisfies organizational requirements while mitigating new quantum threats.

5.3 Difficulties and Obstacles in Implementation

Making the switch to PQC is a complicated process, and there may be a number of difficulties encountered along the way. A successful migration requires an understanding of these difficulties.

Performance bottlenecks and compatibility problems

Integrating PQC algorithms into historical infrastructure might be challenging because they are not always directly compatible with current systems.

- Software and Hardware Compatibility: Classical cryptographic techniques were taken into consideration while designing many of the systems, libraries, and hardware devices that are currently in use. The underlying infrastructure may need to be updated in order to implement PQC; this could entail replacing entire systems, buying new hardware, or rewriting significant amounts of software.

- Performance Issues: PQC algorithms can demand a lot more computing power than classical algorithms, particularly those based on lattices or code-based cryptography. Performance bottlenecks could result from this, especially in systems where speed is crucial, such high-throughput financial systems or real-time communications.

- Larger key sizes are necessary for many PQC algorithms, including those in lattice-based encryption, compared to conventional methods. This can make transmission and storage difficult, particularly for systems that need high-performance, low-latency encryption.

Legacy System Restrictions and Organizational Opposition

Change is frequently resisted by organizations, particularly when it comes to modernizing vital infrastructure. Internal resistance to the PQC migration is possible, especially in companies that have long used the current systems.

- Organizational inertia or unwillingness to adopt new technology may be caused by worries about the expense, complexity, or potential disruption to current operations. The learning curve for new procedures and systems may be resisted by staff members.

- Legacy Systems: A lot of businesses still use antiquated cryptography standards that are incompatible with them. These systems may need to be completely redesigned in order to migrate to PQC, which can be time-consuming and resource-intensive.

5.4 Best Practices and Roadmaps

Organizations must create clear roadmaps and adhere to best practices that guarantee a seamless migration process in order to successfully convert to PQC. This entails developing a strategic strategy that covers each stage of the migration, from planning to execution.

Developing Plans for Phased Migration

A staggered migration plan divides the changeover into smaller, more doable segments. This strategy guarantees that PQC is systematically incorporated throughout the company while reducing risks.

Phase 1: Planning and Assessment: Make a list of all the cryptographic systems that are in use now and evaluate their quantum readiness. Establish the timeframe for PQC adoption and identify the critical areas that require urgent attention.

Phase 2: Implementation Pilot: To test PQC solutions or deploy hybrid cryptography systems, pick a few systems or use cases. Keep an eye on performance, fix any problems, and improve the rollout plan.

Phase 3: Complete Deployment: Start moving important systems toward complete PQC adoption as soon as the pilot phase is completed. Make certain that employees receive training and that any legacy systems are phased out appropriately.

Training and Organizational Policies for PQC Adoption

Organizations must put in place rules that facilitate the migration in order to guarantee the PQC transition's success. This entails implementing new security procedures, educating employees on the new cryptographic systems, and making sure that all legal requirements are met.

- Training Programs: Provide PQC concepts and technology to developers, IT personnel, and decision-makers. To guarantee that everyone is prepared to oversee and execute the new processes, give them practical instruction.

- Compliance and Governance: Verify that the switch to PQC complies with legal and industry norms. Create a governance structure that integrates PQC into the organization's security policy as a whole.

The process of switching to post-quantum cryptography is difficult but essential to securing security systems against the new dangers that quantum computing will bring. Organizations can make the shift by closely evaluating risks, putting hybrid systems into place, overcoming implementation obstacles, and adhering to a planned roadmap.

CHAPTER 6

INDUSTRY USE CASES AND REAL-WORLD APPLICATIONS

There are significant ramifications for many industries as quantum computing emerges as a game-changing technology, especially those that depend on strong cryptographic security measures. This chapter will examine how post-quantum cryptography (PQC), also known as quantum-resistant encryption, is positioned to meet the demands of a number of important sectors. We will talk about how PQC will be put into practice to protect private information, adhere to legal requirements, and preserve national security in the face of new quantum dangers. This chapter offers useful insights into the actual uses of PQC in the real world by examining specific use cases in industries like financial services, healthcare, government, and internet infrastructure.

6.1 Banking and Financial Services

One of the industries where security is crucial is the financial services sector. To secure transactions, safeguard private information, and foster consumer trust, financial institutions mostly rely on encryption. The industry must prioritize the transition to PQC since the emergence of quantum computing creates new vulnerabilities.

Safeguarding Transactions and Private Information

Cryptography is essential to the financial industry for protecting payment systems, internet transactions, and authentication. Elliptic curve cryptography (ECC) and RSA are two popular algorithms used to safeguard communications and stop illegal access. However, methods like Shor's algorithm, which can effectively factor big numbers and solve discrete logarithms, could be used by quantum computers to crack these traditional encryption schemes, destroying RSA and ECC.

Financial institutions need to be ready for the potential for transactions and sensitive data to be attacked as quantum computers advance. PQC provides a way to guarantee the ongoing safety of:

- Customer Accounts: Post-quantum algorithms offer encryption techniques that are impenetrable by quantum computers. Lattice-based encryption systems, like NTRU and Kyber, for instance, are quantum-resistant and can shield client accounts from future illegal access.

- Payments and Transfers: Quantum-resistant cryptographic methods are required to secure money transfers, whether they are made between banks or through credit cards. Updating payment systems that depend on RSA for transaction security is part of this.

- Digital Signatures: Quantum-safe substitutes, such as those based on hash-based or lattice-based cryptography, must replace digital signatures used to authenticate financial contracts, agreements, and transactions.

In order to preserve security in the face of quantum attacks, blockchain technology and cryptocurrencies that rely on safe digital signatures and consensus algorithms will have to switch to PQC.

Regulatory and Compliance Aspects

With stringent regulations pertaining to data protection, transaction transparency, and security standards, the financial services industry is likewise highly regulated. By switching to PQC, security issues will be resolved and adherence to these legal frameworks will be guaranteed. Important rules consist of:

- The General Data Protection Regulation, or GDPR, makes sure that private information is safely encrypted and safeguarded. The current encryption techniques are at risk from quantum computing, hence switching to PQC will be required to meet GDPR's data protection regulations.

- To secure credit card information, financial institutions must adhere to the Payment Card Industry Data Security Standard, or PCI DSS. These standards will need to change in order to include

PQC measures when conventional encryption becomes more susceptible to quantum assaults.

- A regulatory system known as Basel III requires banks to keep sufficient capital buffers to cover risks, including cybersecurity concerns. Financial organizations can protect their cryptographic infrastructure and reduce their exposure to quantum-driven security flaws by implementing PQC.

- Financial institutions will need to update compliance protocols, perform risk assessments, and make sure all systems are quantum-resistant in order to comply with regulatory requirements as a result of the shift to PQC.

6.2 Data privacy and healthcare

Numerous sensitive personal data sets, such as patient records, medical histories, and health insurance information, are handled by the healthcare sector It is crucial to protect the confidentiality and security of this data, particularly as healthcare institutions transition to more digital and networked models. Concerns over the safety of medical records and the possibility that quantum computers could crack existing encryption protocols are becoming more prevalent as the field of quantum computing develops.

Protecting Medical Records in the Quantum Era

The security of medical data is seriously threatened by quantum computing. For example, a quantum computer might be able to send patient data over unsecure lines or decrypt encrypted medical records kept in databases. Medical data confidentiality and integrity must be guaranteed by healthcare systems using PQC solutions:

- Encryption of Patient Data: RSA or AES encryption is currently used to protect patient records that are kept on physical systems or in cloud databases. These encryption systems might be cracked by quantum computing, potentially exposing private health data. Long-term security of health data can be achieved with quantum-resilient encryption solutions provided by PQC algorithms like NTRU and Lizard.

- Telemedicine and Remote Healthcare: As online consultations and telemedicine become more common, it is critical to secure patient-provider communication. PQC can guarantee that medical consultations, digital prescriptions, and video chats are secure and impervious to quantum-based attacks.

- The increasing number of medical equipment that are linked to the internet (IoT) necessitates their protection from cyberattacks. To protect patient safety, firmware updates and device connectivity can be secured using post-quantum cryptography techniques.

Making Sure PQC Complies with HIPAA and GDPR

Apart from security considerations, healthcare institutions have to follow laws like the GDPR in Europe and the Health Insurance Portability and Accountability Act (HIPAA) in the United States. These rules require that patient data be protected and that medical information be handled securely. Healthcare firms can maintain compliance with these strict privacy and data protection standards by implementing PQC.

- HIPAA Compliance: HIPAA mandates that healthcare institutions put in place suitable security measures to secure patient health data. Healthcare providers can comply with these regulations and protect patient privacy in a post-quantum future by using quantum-resistant encryption.

- The GDPR's emphasis on data protection necessitates that healthcare businesses safeguard patient information from unwanted access. PQC can help achieve this goal by protecting private health data from possible quantum attacks.

- Healthcare providers can preserve regulatory compliance, safeguard their systems from new quantum risks, and guarantee the privacy of medical records by implementing PQC.

6.3 Defense and Government

From defense plans to confidential communications, governments and defense organizations are in charge of protecting critical national data. Since many of the encryption techniques currently employed to safeguard sensitive information could be readily cracked by quantum algorithms, the emergence of quantum computing poses an existential threat to national security.

Classified Communications and National Security Priorities

To keep their vital infrastructures safe from quantum threats, governments everywhere are making significant investments in PQC. The stakes are significant in terms of national security. Sensitive operations may be compromised if adversaries with access to quantum computing were able to decipher secret data.

- Encryption is essential for the military's secure communications, which include real-time coordination and satellite broadcasts. These

77

communications must be safeguarded by quantum-resistant algorithms as quantum computers advance in order to maintain the security of military secrets.

- Governments manage vast amounts of sensitive information, such as national defense plans, diplomatic correspondence, and intelligence reports. The repercussions might be catastrophic if quantum assaults were to decipher these data. Even in the face of potential quantum attackers, classified data can be protected by implementing PQC solutions.

- Cybersecurity of Government Systems: Quantum-enabled cyberattacks must be prevented from affecting government systems, such as tax records, citizen data, and public services. By switching to PQC, these systems will be protected against changing threats.

The Value of Early Adoption of PQC

It is impossible to overestimate the significance of early

PQC acceptance for the government and defense. Long before quantum computers pose a real threat, national security organizations need to start making the switch to PQC. In order to upgrade cryptographic systems and safeguard vital infrastructure, this calls for strategic planning and forward-thinking.

- Research and Development: To create quantum-safe encryption techniques that meet their unique requirements, governments must fund PQC research and work with academics and business.

- The development of national cybersecurity frameworks that integrate PQC concepts will contribute to the future security of public sector systems.

6.4 Internet Infrastructure and Cloud Services

The security of internet infrastructure is more important than ever as consumers and organizations depend more and more on the internet for data storage, communication, and commerce. PQC must be integrated into internet services like cloud providers, VPNs, and TLS (Transport Layer Security) in order to preserve data privacy and guarantee ongoing security in the post-quantum era.

How Cloud Providers, VPNs, and TLS Are Including PQC

- TLS Encryption: RSA and ECC are used for key exchange and encryption in TLS, the protocol that secures the majority of internet traffic. Quantum computers have the potential to violate these norms as their power increases. Therefore, to guarantee the long-term security of web traffic, PQC integration into TLS is crucial. To secure TLS communications, algorithms such as Kyber and NTRU are already undergoing testing for application in hybrid cryptographic schemes.

- VPNs: RSA and ECC are also essential for encryption in virtual private networks, which are used to protect internet connections. To guarantee that these connections stay private even after the development of quantum computing, PQC integration is the key to the future of VPN security.

- Cloud Services: As more companies store data on the cloud, it is essential to make sure that this data is secure. PQC solutions are already being investigated by cloud providers to safeguard private information kept in cloud infrastructures. Cloud providers like Google Cloud and Amazon Web Services (AWS) are now investigating ways to integrate post-quantum cryptography into their products.

The Function of Digital Identity and Certificate Authorities

- The task of providing digital certificates that authenticate internet entities falls to the Certificate Authorities (CAs). CAs must use PQC to make sure that their certificates are impenetrable to quantum adversaries in order to be safe in a quantum future.

- Digital Identity: Verifying one's identity online is becoming a crucial security issue as more individuals trade online. PQC is able to secure identity authentication techniques, guaranteeing that credentials and personal information are shielded against quantum attacks.

Industry-wide adoption of PQC will be essential to preserving data security, privacy, and compliance as quantum computing poses new difficulties. PQC provides a means to safeguard sensitive data in a post-quantum environment and guard against the nascent quantum threat, whether in the financial services, healthcare, government, or internet infrastructure sectors. PQC has many practical uses, and early adoption will be essential for businesses to stay ahead of the curve and protect their most valuable assets

CHAPTER 7

Post-Quantum Cryptography in the Developer Ecosystem

Post-quantum cryptography (PQC) is becoming increasingly necessary across many businesses as the quantum era draws near. However, cryptographers and security experts are not the only ones responsible for the shift to quantum-resistant encryption. Developers, who are essential to the development of software systems and applications, also need to be knowledgeable about PQC. With an emphasis on tools, libraries, language-specific implementations, testing, and community resources, this chapter examines how developers might interact with PQC.

We shall examine the following in this chapter:

1. Toolkits and Libraries
2. Language-Specific Implementations
3. Validation and Testing

4. Education and Community for Developers

7.1 Toolkits and Libraries

Using libraries and toolkits is one of the most effective ways to incorporate post-quantum cryptography into programs. Without having to start from scratch, these open-source tools make it easier to construct PQC algorithms. They frequently have a strong community, are always changing, and are designed to function well on various platforms.

Open-Source Tools such as PQClean and Open Quantum Safe (OQS)

Open Quantum Safe (OQS) and PQClean are two well-known open-source initiatives in the PQC field that give programmers the resources they require to include quantum-resistant algorithms into their applications.

OQS (Open Quantum Safe): A project called Open Quantum secure aims to provide cryptographic algorithms that are secure at the quantum level. It contains a number of libraries that have quantum-attack-resistant algorithms as Kyber, NTRU, and others. Developers may quickly experiment with and incorporate quantum-safe encryption into their apps thanks to OQS's user-friendly toolkit.

Additionally, the project includes a reference implementation with an interface akin to that of current cryptography libraries (like OpenSSL). For developers who need to start utilizing PQC but are already accustomed to normal cryptographic APIs, this facilitates the transition.

By connecting with the OQS library, developers may incorporate PQC algorithms straight into applications, enabling them to use quantum-safe encryption in addition to conventional techniques. Wide compatibility is ensured by the library's support for popular operating systems like Windows, Linux, and macOS.

OQS also places a strong emphasis on hybrid cryptography, which blends PQC with conventional methods. Developers may make the shift to a completely quantum safe future more gradually thanks to this hybrid method, which keeps systems safe from both classical and quantum threats.

Another essential library in the PQC ecosystem is PQClean, which aims to provide post-quantum cryptography algorithm implementations that are clean, performant, and compliant with standards. It focuses on solutions that are efficient and lightweight, making them appropriate for situations with constraints such as embedded systems and Internet of Things devices.

Algorithm Selection: PQClean is compatible with a number of post-quantum encryption techniques, such as multivariate quadratic equations, code-based, and lattice-based. It guarantees that developers are utilizing the most recent and standardized techniques by providing implementations that adhere to the algorithms being tested for the NIST PQC standardization process.

Optimized Performance: When incorporating new cryptographic algorithms into applications, developers place a high value on performance. By offering performance benchmarks, PQClean assists developers in determining which algorithms are most suited for their use case and in comprehending the computational cost of each approach.

How Applications Can Use PQC Algorithms

Although there are certain special considerations, integrating PQC algorithms into applications is comparable to integrating typical cryptography libraries:

- Changing the Cryptographic Suite: Post-quantum algorithms can be used by developers in place of more traditional encryption techniques like RSA or ECC. This can be accomplished modularly, enabling developers to use hybrid approaches that blend classical and quantum-resistant algorithms to progressively integrate PQC.

- Backward Compatibility Testing: Developers should make sure that the PQC implementation is compatible with current systems because the majority of systems are based on traditional cryptographic protocols. Backward compatibility can be provided via hybrid encryption methods, which combine post-quantum and conventional algorithms.

- Security Audits: To make sure the algorithms are implemented correctly and safely, thorough security audits must be conducted on the PQC integration, just like with any cryptographic implementation.

7.2 Implementations Specific to Languages

Every programming language has advantages, and PQC adoption will differ depending on the language environment. While some languages rely on external libraries to provide cryptographic functionality, others include built-in support for cryptographic libraries. To use these quantum-safe algorithms efficiently, developers must be aware of how to implement PQC in different languages.

PQC Support for Rust, Go, Python, and C

In system-level and embedded development, where memory management and efficiency are crucial, C is still one of the most popular programming languages. OpenSSL and other cryptographic libraries developed for C are being modified to enable PQC algorithms like NTRU and Kyber.

Use Case: PQC algorithms can be integrated by developers utilizing libraries like Open Quantum Safe while creating operating systems, security tools, or network protocols in C.

Performance: Because of its low-level capabilities, C is appropriate for applications like secure communications or real-time systems that demand high-performance cryptography.

Python: Python is a popular language in data science, web development, and research where usability and speed are key considerations. To incorporate PQC, Python writers can utilize libraries such as PyCryptodome or PyCryptor. By providing Python bindings for quantum-resistant algorithms, these libraries enable programmers to take advantage of Python's advantages without compromising security.

Use Case: Python is perfect for creating cryptography modules for data science applications, prototyping quantum-safe systems, and incorporating PQC into web frameworks for safe online applications.

Performance: Python is perfect for situations where development speed is important and performance requirements are less strict, even though it might not be as quick as C for cryptographic operations.

Rust is becoming more and more well-liked due to its memory safety features, which make it a great option for applications that are sensitive to security. Rust-PQC is one of several ongoing projects aimed at giving Rust developers access to quantum-resistant cryptographic solutions.

Use Case: When memory safety and parallelism are critical, Rust is a great option for secure web servers, cryptographic libraries, or blockchain technologies.

Rust is a powerful language for creating high-performance, quantum-resistant systems since its performance is comparable to that of C.

Go: Popular for cloud-based and networking applications, Go (or Golang) is renowned for its concurrency and scalability. Developers can include PQC into their applications while preserving Go's speed and ease of use with the help of libraries like Go-PQC.

Go is perfect for creating microservices or scalable cloud services that need secure, quantum-safe connections.

Performance: Go is a suitable choice for high-performance cryptographic operations in web-based or networked applications because it strikes a compromise between usability and speed.

Performance Benchmarks and Use Cases

The language and particular algorithm utilized determine the performance benchmarks for PQC algorithms. The algorithm and language combination that best suits the developers' performance and security requirements must be carefully considered.

For instance, when implemented in C, Python, Rust, or Go, lattice-based cryptographic algorithms like Kyber and NTRU may have varying computational requirements, although potentially providing a reasonable security-performance balance.

7.3 Validation and Testing

Cryptographic algorithm implementation is a risky business because any mistake could result in security flaws. In order to guarantee that PQC algorithms are accurate and resistant to both classical and quantum attacks, testing and validation are essential.

Guaranteeing the Correctness and Attack Resistance of Algorithms

Any PQC algorithm must pass stringent testing to ensure its accuracy and security before being implemented in a production setting. This comprises:

- Correctness: Verifying that the algorithm executes

safe key exchanges or signatures and encrypts and decrypts data appropriately.

- The ability of algorithms to withstand known classical and quantum attacks must be verified. Analysis against such attacks is part of this.

Chosen Ciphertext Attack (CCA)

- Side-channel Attacks
- Lattice Attacks
- Chosen Plaintext Attack (CPA) (exclusive to cryptography based on lattices)

Certifications and Standard Testing Frameworks

- The NIST PQC Standardization is as follows: PQC algorithm standardization has been a long-term project of the National Institute of Standards and Technology (NIST). To make sure that their systems adhere to the most recent standards, developers should choose and implement PQC algorithms in accordance with NIST's recommendations and guidelines.

- Certification and Audits: Developers should think about third-party certification for their implementations to further confirm the algorithm's integrity. Cryptographic modules can undergo certification procedures from organizations like Common Criteria to verify that they adhere to strict security requirements.

7.4 Community and Education for Developers

Adopting PQC in the developer ecosystem necessitates a thorough comprehension of the underlying concepts and algorithms in addition to having access to the appropriate tools. The tools accessible to developers to assist them in navigating the post-quantum cryptography landscape are covered in this section.

Documentation, Training Materials, and Engaging Communities

A range of resources are available for developers to learn about PQC:

PQC modules are frequently included in quantum computing and cryptography courses offered by numerous universities and online learning environments.

Documentation: Developers need well-maintained documentation. Libraries such as PQClean and Open Quantum Safe include comprehensive usage examples and documentation.

Conferences and Workshops: Developers can stay current on the most recent findings and developments in PQC by attending conferences like as QCrypt or NIST workshops.

Establishing a Secure PQC Developer Pipeline

Developers must be a part of a community that prioritizes security. Creating a safe pipeline entails:

Regular Security Audits: To find vulnerabilities early in the development process, perform routine code audits and use automated testing techniques.

Collaborating with the larger developer community via open-source projects, GitHub repositories, and forums

Contributions facilitate the sharing of best practices and keep developers informed.

Developers will be better equipped to incorporate PQC into their projects and guarantee the security of their apps in a post-quantum future if they remain involved with the community and pursue ongoing education.

For developers wishing to integrate post-quantum cryptography into their systems, this chapter offers a thorough manual. Developers need to be proactive and knowledgeable in order to get ready for the quantum era, from knowing the tools and libraries to making sure that testing is thorough and interacting with the community

CHAPTER 8

Quantum-Safe Alternatives and Quantum Key Distribution

In the field of cybersecurity, the emergence of quantum computing offers both tremendous benefits and formidable obstacles. Quantum Key Distribution (QKD) and post-quantum cryptography (PQC) are two of the most talked-about subjects at the nexus of quantum computing and cryptography. Although they both seek to protect communications from impending quantum threats, their strategies and real-world applications are different. This chapter examines these two paradigms, contrasting their advantages and disadvantages and considering potential future collaborations.

This chapter will discuss:

1. Quantum Key Distribution (QKD): An Overview
2. QKD vs. PQC: Do They Complement or Compete?

3. QKD's Practical Limitations

4. Emerging Hybrid Security Models

8.1 Quantum Key Distribution (QKD): An Overview

A method for safely exchanging cryptographic keys over a potentially insecure communication channel is called quantum key distribution, or QKD. The distinctive feature of QKD is that it uses the ideas of quantum mechanics to offer security, which is essentially distinct from traditional cryptography techniques.

QKD Fundamentals and How They Vary from PQC

Enabling two parties to share a secret key without worrying about it being intercepted or eavesdropped on is the main objective of QKD. This is accomplished by encoding information using quantum bits (qubits) and the polarization and other quantum characteristics of light.

The Workings of Quantum Mechanics:

The Heisenberg Uncertainty Principle and quantum entanglement are fundamental to QKD. According to the uncertainty principle, interception is detectable because measuring a quantum particle's position or momentum, for example, affects it in some manner. This implies that any effort to intercept the quantum key will cause the system to malfunction and notify the persons involved in the communication.

The Function of Quantum Channels:

A communication channel that transmits quantum information is called a quantum channel. These could be satellite links, free space, or fiber-optic cables. Quantum bits, or qubits, are carried via these channels and are usually encoded in photon polarization. The fundamental characteristic of quantum communication is that interception is detectable as the qubits cannot be duplicated or measured without causing them to be disturbed.

The goal of post-quantum cryptography (PQC) algorithms, in contrast, is to secure communications through the use of traditional techniques that are impervious to attacks by quantum computing. PQC concentrates on creating cryptographic algorithms that are resistant to the processing power of quantum computers, whereas QKD exploits the physical characteristics of quantum mechanics to secure key distribution.

For safe key exchange over possibly insecure channels, QKD is especially well-suited.

The goal of PQC is to substitute algorithms that are impervious to quantum assaults for conventional cryptography systems like RSA and ECC.

Quantum Channels and the BB84 Protocol

Charles Bennett and Gilles Brassard proposed BB84, one of the most famous QKD systems, in 1984. The transmission of quantum bits (qubits) recorded in one of four potential polarization states forms the foundation of the BB84 protocol. The receiver decodes the key using a matching measurement basis after these states are transmitted over a quantum channel, usually with photons.

Photon Polarization: Information can be represented by the polarization of photons. For instance, a "1" could be represented by one polarization and a "0" by another. Any interception can be detected because of the quantum nature of these photons, which prevent an eavesdropper from measuring them without interfering with the system.

BB84 Protocol Security:

Because any eavesdropping on the quantum channel will result in visible mistakes in the transmitted key, BB84 is secure. The integrity of the key can be guaranteed by the parties using an error correction technique after it has been transferred, but the existence of an eavesdropper will cause discernible differences.

8.2 Is PQC and QKD a Competition or Complement?

The future of secure communications depends on both post-quantum cryptography (PQC) and quantum key distribution (QKD), but the question is whether we should pick one over the other or if they can work in tandem.

Comparative Advantages and Disadvantages

- One of QKD's benefits is its unconditional security. The main advantage of QKD is that it is based on the rules of physics rather than mathematical conjecture.

A theoretically indestructible degree of security is provided by QKD, provided that the laws of quantum physics remain valid.

- Taking Quantum Threats Head-on: Because QKD employs quantum mechanical concepts that are impervious to quantum attacks, it is especially made to handle the security threats presented by quantum computers.

The following are some of QKD's disadvantages:

- Infrastructure Requirements: Specialized infrastructure, such as quantum repeaters and channels (fiber optics or satellite links), which are still in the early stages of development, are needed to set up a quantum key distribution system. Because of this, QKD is costly and challenging to scale for general use.

- Limitations on Distance: Currently, the loss of quantum information during channel transmission limits the effective implementation distance of QKD. Even while efforts to increase this distance are still in progress, there are still many obstacles to be addressed.

The following are some benefits of PQC:

- Scalability: PQC algorithms can be included into current communication systems, including VPNs or SSL/TLS for secure online browsing, without necessitating major infrastructure modifications.

- Adaptability: Post-quantum cryptography offers long-term security even as quantum computing advances and may be used in a range of systems, including embedded devices and public-key infrastructures.

One of PQC's disadvantages is its computational overhead. Compared to more conventional cryptographic techniques like RSA or ECC, some post-quantum algorithms, particularly those based on lattices, require greater processing power. Particularly in areas with limitations, this could result in decreased performance and increased energy usage.

Which Use Cases Are Best for Each Method?

QKD Use Cases:

- High-Security Communication: QKD is perfect for applications in the military, financial institutions, and government where complete security is crucial.

- Secure Key Exchange: QKD is helpful when a secure key exchange is required and a classical approach (such as RSA or ECC) is thought to be susceptible to future quantum attacks.

The following are examples of PQC use cases:

- General-Purpose Cryptography: Post-quantum cryptographic algorithms are more appropriate for general-purpose applications, like protecting email correspondence, cloud storage, and web traffic.

- Embedded and IoT Devices: PQC is better suitable for a larger variety of devices that might not be able to handle QKD because it can be included into systems with constrained resources.

PQC provides a workable way to future-proof cryptographic systems, whereas QKD delivers unmatched security based on quantum physics. Although the two strategies can play complementary roles in the developing field of quantum-safe cryptography, they are not necessarily rivals.

8.3 QKD's Practical Restrictions

Although QKD offers theoretical security benefits, its practical drawbacks have hindered its broad use.

Infrastructure, Scalability, and Cost Issues

- High Costs: A QKD system's implementation necessitates a significant investment in specialized infrastructure and hardware, including photon sources and quantum repeaters. The scalability of QKD for large-scale deployments is constrained by the high development and maintenance costs of these systems.

- One of the biggest challenges is scaling up QKD systems to span bigger geographic areas or networks. Long-distance signal loss occurs with quantum channels, and although efforts are being made to create quantum repeaters that can magnify quantum signals over longer distances, this technology is still in its infancy.

Physical Vulnerabilities and Trust Models

- Trust Models: To control key distribution, QKD systems frequently rely on relay points or trusted nodes in the network. If an enemy manages to hack these trusted nodes, their security could become a weakness. Furthermore, QKD equipment must be physically secure; any tampering or physical attacks could compromise the security of the entire system.

- Physical Vulnerabilities: Attacks like hacking or physical interception could target the physical infrastructure that supports QKD, such as satellite links or optical fibers. Although maintaining the security of these networks is crucial, doing so presents several practical difficulties.

8.4 New Models of Hybrid Security

Given the drawbacks of both PQC and QKD, hybrid models that incorporate the advantages of both strategies could be the way of the future for secure communications.

Combining Post-Quantum Systems with QKD

- Hybrid security models would combine PQC algorithms to offer strong encryption and authentication with QKD for the safe exchange of cryptographic keys. Even though quantum computers are not yet strong enough to compromise current systems, such a concept may provide quantum-safe security.

- Hybrid Encryption: QKD may be utilized in these hybrid systems to safely exchange post-quantum or conventional cryptographic keys. An additional degree of security can be added by using post-quantum encryption methods with the keys after they have been safely exchanged via QKD.

Moving Ahead with Layered Quantum-Safe Structures

- Layered architectures create multifaceted protection systems by combining QKD and quantum-safe cryptography. Multiple security protocol levels (such as encryption, authentication, and key exchange) would cooperate in such systems to provide all-encompassing defense against both conventional and quantum threats.

- End-to-End Security: By using a layered approach, security may be preserved at all communication levels, from the application layer to the physical layer, offering end-to-end protection.

Redundancy: The application

Redundancy is created by using numerous security methods, guaranteeing that protection will still be provided even in the event that one is compromised.

There are a lot of practical obstacles to overcome even though Quantum Key Distribution (QKD) presents an intriguing new avenue for quantum-safe communication. Not all quantum hazards are addressed by post-quantum cryptography (PQC), while it provides a more scalable solution. As we move into the quantum future, hybrid models that combine QKD and PQC might offer the most promising way forward, guaranteeing that communication stays safe

CHAPTER 9

ETHICAL CONSIDERATIONS, REGULATION, AND POLICY

The ramifications of quantum computing for cybersecurity get increasingly complicated as it develops. In addition to the technical difficulties of moving toward quantum-safe systems, the ethical, legal, and policy environments are changing simultaneously. Addressing the new risks and opportunities that quantum technologies provide is the responsibility of government departments, global organizations, and business executives. Furthermore, how we strike a balance between the advantages of quantum developments and respect for security, privacy, and sovereignty depends heavily on ethical issues.

9.1 The World of Policies

A global discussion on cybersecurity standards and governance has been sparked by the emergence of quantum computing and the pressing need for quantum-safe encryption methods. The role of governments and international organizations in establishing regulations to guarantee the safe and just application of quantum technology is growing.

International Cooperation and Government Requirements

In order to guarantee that quantum computing and quantum encryption are used in ways that preserve economic interests, foster innovation, and protect national security, countries are developing laws and regulatory frameworks as these technologies advance.

National Strategies: Governments everywhere are acting to lessen the dangers that quantum threats represent to vital infrastructure, such as defense systems, financial systems, and communication networks. For example, the National Quantum Initiative Act (2018) in the US mandates that government agencies give priority to research and development of quantum computing, including measures to fortify cybersecurity against assaults enabled by quantum technology.

International Agreements and Standards: Due to the worldwide ramifications of quantum computing, international cooperation is required. Nations are becoming more conscious of the fact that international norms and frameworks, in addition to their own domestic laws, will determine their capacity to safeguard confidential data. Global cooperation is the key to ensuring that quantum advancements are used responsibly, and multinational organizations such as the World Economic Forum and the United Nations have started holding talks on the moral application of quantum technologies.

Strategic Partnerships: The development of quantum technology has relied heavily on collaborations between governments, academic institutions, and commercial businesses. International cooperation is encouraged by joint projects like the European Quantum Flagship Program, which aims to speed up the study and creation of quantum-safe cryptography. By reducing the dangers, these initiatives guarantee that the advantages of quantum computing may be experienced globally.

The function of agencies such as NIST, NSA, and ENISA

By providing frameworks, certifications, and standards for quantum-safe cybersecurity activities, a number of organizations significantly influence the policy landscape surrounding quantum computing.

The European Union Agency for Cybersecurity, or ENISA, offers thorough guidelines for protecting information systems and networks from new dangers, such as those posed by quantum computing. One of the agency's responsibilities is to advise EU member states on how to include quantum-safe procedures and make sure that vital infrastructure is ready for the hazards of the quantum era.

The National Security Agency (NSA):
In particular, when it comes to planning for quantum threats, the NSA plays a crucial role in directing the US cybersecurity posture. In order to protect against potential quantum decryption capabilities, the NSA has released guidelines for incorporating quantum-resistant algorithms and protocols into current encryption systems.

One of the most important groups in the creation of quantum-safe cryptography standards is NIST (National Institute of Standards and Technology). In order to develop a strong suite of cryptographic solutions to safeguard communications in the quantum era, NIST is assessing and choosing algorithms that can withstand quantum attacks through its Post-Quantum Cryptography Standardization project. Since the cryptographic methods that NIST supports will be the industry standard for guaranteeing secure communications, their position is very important.

9.2 Consequences for Privacy in the Quantum Era

As quantum computing develops, the privacy landscape changes significantly. Data privacy is seriously threatened by quantum computing's capacity to crack popular encryption schemes. It will be necessary to carefully examine sovereignty, privacy regulations, and cross-border difficulties in order to address these concerns.

Problems with Cross-Border Encryption and Data Sovereignty

Making sure that private information is safe across borders is one of the key problems that quantum computing presents. Data sovereignty the notion that data should remain under the jurisdiction of the country in which it originates becomes even more important as national security concerns increase and data moves throughout the world.

The following are some quantum threats to global encryption:

Modern cryptographic systems, like RSA and ECC, rely on the difficulty of solving discrete logarithm issues or factoring huge integers. However, compared to classical computers, quantum computers could handle these issues at an enormously faster rate. Therefore, encryption used to protect sensitive cross-border operations, such as financial transactions, government communications, and personal data, could be readily cracked by quantum computing.

Cross-Border Encryption Laws: Different nations have different privacy and data encryption laws and regulations. These rules need to change in the quantum era to take new cryptographic realities into consideration. To guarantee that international data protection regimes continue to be safe from quantum attacks, it will probably be necessary to develop international treaties or agreements. For example, in order to secure the data of European residents in a world of quantum computing, the General Data Protection Regulation (GDPR) of the European Union may need to be revised to include quantum-safe encryption.

Juggling Individual Rights with Surveillance

In the area of monitoring, quantum technologies can pose moral dilemmas. State and non-state actors could abuse quantum computers' ability to decipher previously encrypted communications for spying.

Issues with Surveillance:
Governments might be tempted to use quantum decryption technology for surveillance, keeping an unprecedented eye on people's communications and activities. Particularly in nations with lax privacy laws or where authoritarian regimes control digital infrastructure, the possibility of widespread surveillance raises questions regarding civil

liberties and individual freedoms.

Ethical Conundrums:

How to strike a balance between individual rights protection and state security is a basic ethical conundrum. Although quantum computing could protect against malevolent cyberattacks, it could also provide governments the ability to eavesdrop on populations, infringing on their right to privacy and freedom. Strict laws and ethical standards must be established to guarantee that quantum innovations are applied sensibly.

9.3 Quantum-Resistant Red Teaming and Ethical Hacking

Cybersecurity experts need to change how they evaluate threats as quantum technologies develop. Red teaming and ethical hacking are essential techniques for finding weaknesses and evaluating how reliable quantum-resistant systems are.

Ethical Hacking Techniques That Are Quantum-Safe

Because they can find flaws before bad actors can take advantage of them, ethical hackers, often known as "white-hat" hackers, are essential to system security. Ethical hackers must use quantum-safe techniques in their penetration testing and security audits since quantum computing opens up new attack avenues.

Quantum Penetration Testing: To evaluate the robustness of an organization's security infrastructure, ethical hackers need to be taught in quantum-safe cryptographic protocols. This could entail confirming the application of post-quantum cryptography methods and assessing the vulnerability of current encryption systems to quantum assaults.

It will be necessary to adapt red team exercises, which involve ethical hackers simulating system attacks, to incorporate quantum opponents. In order to help companies comprehend the possible effects of quantum computing on their security posture, this entails simulating attacks on key infrastructure that are enabled by quantum technology.

Modeling Quantum Opponents

One essential technique for getting businesses ready for quantum threats is simulating quantum adversaries. Quantum adversaries may be able to decipher encrypted data faster than current defenses since they are not constrained by the same computational constraints as classical attackers. By using tools and methods that imitate the capabilities of quantum computing, ethical hackers can create a realistic image of potential risks by simulating quantum adversaries.

Quantum-Resistant Systems Stress Testing:

To be sure that quantum-resistant algorithms can withstand possible quantum decryption attacks, ethical hackers need to devise methods for stress-testing them. Organizations can evaluate the efficacy of their defenses and make the required adjustments prior to the widespread adoption of quantum computing by modeling adversaries with quantum capabilities.

9.4 PQC Accessibility and the Digital Divide

Although quantum technologies have a lot of promise, there are many obstacles in the way of the widespread adoption of quantum-safe cryptography solutions. Accessible technology solutions and careful policymaking are necessary to guarantee that small enterprises and developing nations are not left behind in the quantum era.

Making Sure Developing Countries and Small Businesses Don't Get Left Behind

Adoption of quantum-safe encryption may be hampered by substantial financial and technological obstacles for small businesses and developing countries. For companies with little funding, the expenses of deploying post-quantum cryptography solutions, such as updating infrastructure and implementing new protocols, may be unaffordable.

Global Standards and Support: Promoting worldwide collaboration and creating global standards that enable universal access to quantum-safe cryptography are two ways to resolve these discrepancies. To encourage small businesses and impoverished countries in their efforts to switch to quantum-safe technologies, governments and huge organizations must work together. This can entail offering access to open-source solutions, financial incentives, and technical assistance.

Low-Cost Solutions and Open-Source Support

Encouraging Open-Source Solutions: Adoption of quantum-safe encryption can be greatly aided by open-source software and cryptographic techniques. The international community can guarantee that quantum-resistant systems are available to everyone, irrespective of financial or technological constraints, by encouraging open-source development and cooperation.

Low-Cost Implementation: As quantum technologies advance, there is a growing demand for inexpensive solutions that are simple to implement in settings with limited resources. By funding research and providing incentives for the development of scalable, reasonably priced cryptography systems, governments and international organizations can contribute to the advancement of affordable quantum safe technologies.

There are many potential and difficulties at the nexus of ethics, regulation, and policy in the quantum era. Leaders in the business sector, governments, and international organizations must collaborate to design frameworks that support responsible quantum development while preserving individual rights, privacy, and security. It is crucial that no one is left behind as the quantum revolution takes place, particularly small businesses and underdeveloped countries, so that everyone may take advantage of quantum-safe cryptography

CHAPTER 10

THE FUTURE OF CYBERSECURITY IN A POST-QUANTUM WORLD

The future of cybersecurity is developing in ways that are both fascinating and challenging as we stand on the brink of the quantum revolution. Although quantum computing has great promise for the future, it also carries a number of hitherto unheard-of concerns, especially with regard to the security of digital data. Long regarded as the cornerstone of contemporary cybersecurity, the current cryptographic techniques are now in danger of becoming outdated due to quantum developments.

This chapter explores cybersecurity in the post-quantum era, looking at current research, quantum-resilient architectures, the effect on digital trust, and how to create a quantum-safe society. The broader effects of quantum computing on international security, confidence in digital networks, and our collective readiness for a new cybersecurity era will all be taken into account as we examine these subjects.

We'll investigate:

The following are some of the long-term effects on trust and digital identity:

1. Continuous Research and Future Algorithms.
2. Quantum-Resilient Architectures
3. Creating a Quantum-Safe Society

10.1 Current Studies and Upcoming Algorithms

Significant difficulties in the field of encryption arise in the quantum age. The cryptography methods that safeguard everything from national security to online banking may be compromised if quantum computers become more potent. Researchers from all across the world are working to create post-quantum cryptography (PQC), or cryptographic algorithms that remain safe even in a world driven by quantum technology, in order to overcome these issues.

Innovations and Trials in Next-Generation PQC

Organizations like the National Institute of Standards and Technology (NIST) are at the forefront of the ongoing race to create quantum-safe algorithms. Launched in 2016, NIST's Post-Quantum Cryptography Standardization Project seeks to assess, standardize, and apply cryptographic algorithms that are resistant to attacks by quantum computing. Before quantum computers pose a threat to the actual world, the objective is to replace current cryptographic protocols with ones that are resistant to quantum errors.

Proposals for Algorithms:

Lattice-based cryptography, hash-based signatures, code-based cryptography, and multivariate quadratic equations are some of the most promising options for post-quantum cryptography. Unlike the popular RSA and ECC algorithms, which are easily cracked by Shor's algorithm on a quantum machine, these approaches rely on mathematical difficulties that are challenging for quantum computers to solve.

Lattice-based cryptography:

The most advanced methods for quantum-resistant cryptography are thought to be lattice-based techniques. These systems depend on the difficulty of high-dimensional lattice problems, such the Shortest Vector Problem (SVP), which is a challenge for quantum computers. Digital signatures, key exchange protocols, and encryption might all be implemented using lattice-based cryptography.

Hash-Based Signatures: Post-quantum applications are also investigating hash-based signature techniques. By using hash functions, these systems generate safe digital signatures that are impenetrable by quantum algorithms. Although they provide protection against quantum threats, issues with key size and signature efficiency may arise.

Cryptography Based on Codes:
Another interesting approach is code-based cryptography, which depends on the difficulty of decoding specific error-correcting codes. Despite being in use for many years, this approach has recently gained renewed attention because of its quantum resistance.

Verification and Testing:

Making sure the new algorithms are efficient and safe is one of the most difficult problems in this field. To make sure these algorithms can survive attacks from both classical and quantum opponents, researchers are putting them to the test against quantum simulators. Extensive testing is necessary to make sure these algorithms are robust and scalable as we get closer to standardizing them.

Getting Ready for Unexpected Quantum Power

Even while PQC research is progressing rapidly, it's crucial to remember that quantum computing is still in its early stages. The full potential of quantum machines is hard to foresee, and some theorists contend that we might be underestimating them. Because of this uncertainty, cybersecurity needs to be ready for unforeseen quantum advances in addition to relying on current research.

QML stands for Quantum Machine Learning.
A new area of study that examines the relationship between machine learning and quantum computing is called quantum machine learning. Quantum computers have the

potential to break existing encryption methods or speed up the creation of new ones if they can be included into machine learning systems. With the emergence of QML, cybersecurity professionals need to be on the lookout for such advancements and implement quantum-resilient tactics.

Assimilation of Novel Quantum Algorithms:

The difficulty lies not just in creating quantum-safe algorithms but also in predicting novel quantum algorithms that might surpass current forecasts. To keep abreast of quantum developments, whether in cryptography or quantum-enhanced hacking methods, ongoing study is required.

10.2 Architectures with Quantum Resilience

In the post-quantum era, creating safe systems involves more than merely swapping the algorithms. We need to create quantum-resilient systems that can withstand cyberattacks driven by quantum technology while preserving security, scalability, and performance in a variety of industries.

Creating Long-Term Secure Infrastructure

Forward-thinking infrastructure is necessary for long-term security. From the hardware layer to the software layer, the next generation of digital infrastructure needs to be constructed with quantum resilience in mind.

Quantum-Resilient Hardware: In order to support quantum-safe encryption techniques, hardware systems will need to change. For instance, large quantum-resistant keys must be able to be stored and distributed by cryptographic key management systems, which are essential for data protection. Furthermore, PQC algorithms must be integrated into hardware-based security modules, such as Hardware Security Modules (HSMs), without sacrificing performance.

Cloud Security Post-Quantum:
Cloud service providers must incorporate quantum-resistant protocols since cloud services are now the foundation of contemporary IT infrastructures. Using quantum-safe methods to encrypt data in transit, guarantee

secure communication, and safeguard private data kept in the cloud should be part of post-quantum cloud security.

It is necessary to upgrade end-to-end encryption to quantum-safe protocols (End-to-End Quantum-Safe Protocols). This covers systems for safe data storage, transfer, and access control. It will be necessary to replace conventional encryption methods that are susceptible to quantum assaults, such as Transport Layer Security (TLS), with quantum-safe substitutes.

Going Beyond Algorithms: Regulations, Instruction, and Knowledge

Creating quantum-safe algorithms and structures is essential, but the post-quantum future also necessitates changing laws and raising public awareness.

The implementation of policies that prioritize the shift to quantum-safe systems requires cooperation between governments and industry. These regulations must provide guidelines for quantum-resilient systems, require frequent security assessments, and guarantee that businesses implement post-quantum security measures as a component of their digital transformation.

Education and Workforce Development: As quantum computing advances, the cybersecurity workforce must also change. Universities and research centers must provide specialized courses that give experts the skills they need to create and apply quantum-safe solutions. Experts in cybersecurity must also receive training in order to recognize and reduce the hazards related to quantum technology.

10.3 Long-Term Effects on Digital Identity and Trust

Fundamental ideas of identity and trust are being seriously questioned in a world where quantum computers can crack conventional cryptography techniques. In the digital age, cybersecurity will need to change not just in terms of algorithms but also in how we handle trust.

Reevaluating Models of Digital Trust

Strong encryption is essential to digital trust, which

supports everything from government services to online commerce. New frameworks that take into consideration how quantum computing can threaten current security paradigms will be necessary to preserve this confidence in the post-quantum era.

Quantum-Resilient Trust Models: Quantum-safe technology must be included into new digital trust models. The focus of these models will be zero-trust architectures, in which end-to-end encryption that is resistant to quantum decryption and stringent verification procedures are included into every aspect of the system, from the network to the individual device.

Restoring Confidence in a Quantum Universe:
As quantum computing develops and the flaws in existing systems are revealed, there can be a brief decline in trust. Rebuilding trust will need governments and organizations to be transparent about how they deploy quantum-safe systems and protect digital assets.

Secure Identities, Blockchain, and Authentication

Many cybersecurity solutions, from bitcoin transactions to online identity verification, are based on blockchain and digital identity systems. To stay safe from quantum threats in the post-quantum world, these systems will need to be modified.

The development of quantum-safe protocols is necessary for blockchain systems, which mostly rely on cryptographic algorithms. To preserve the integrity of blockchain data, this can entail switching from elliptic curve signatures to lattice-based or hash-based techniques.

Quantum-Resilient Authentication: Multi-factor authentication (MFA) and other authentication systems need to change to meet the demands of the quantum age. Identity verification will require new protocols, maybe including quantum-resilient digital signatures, to guarantee security even in the face of quantum-powered attacks.

10.4 Establishing a Society Safe by Quantum

The entire civilization must shift to a quantum-safe infrastructure if it is to prosper in a future driven by quantum technology. Close cooperation between a variety of sectors, including government, academia, and industry, will be necessary for this.

Partnerships Between Governments, Industry, and Academic Institutions

Achieving a quantum-safe society requires a concerted effort from all sectors. Governments, universities, and business executives working together can speed up research and development and make sure that we are all ready for the opportunities and challenges presented by quantum technologies.

Public-Private Partnerships: By providing subsidies and R&D assistance, governments can encourage private sector businesses to invest in quantum-safe technologies. At the same time, businesses can help create practical, scalable applications for quantum-safe solutions.

International Cooperation: International cooperation is crucial due to the worldwide nature of quantum computing. To establish international standards, exchange research results, and apply quantum-safe solutions internationally, nations must cooperate.

A Change in Culture to Proactive Cybersecurity

A mental shift from reactive to proactive cybersecurity will be necessary as society moves toward quantum-safe technology. Security at every stage of digital contact must be a top priority for both individuals and companies as quantum risks become more real.

Promoting Quantum Awareness: Cybersecurity education needs to reach the general population as well as technical specialists. People will be better equipped to make judgments regarding their digital security if they are aware of the possible dangers posed by quantum technologies and the necessity of quantum-safe solutions.

Proactive Risk Management: Risk management techniques will need to change in the post-quantum era to account for the hazards posed by quantum computing. Institutions must, even in the absence of full-scale quantum computers, start incorporating quantum-safe solutions into their cybersecurity plans now.

Looking ahead, cybersecurity in a post-quantum world presents both challenges and opportunities. Quantum computing has enormous potential to transform industries and advance our knowledge of the cosmos. To protect our most sensitive data, we must, however, reevaluate how we secure our digital lives and construct the necessary infrastructure. We can create a quantum-safe society that can endure future challenges while maintaining the trust that underpins our digital interactions by embracing innovation and working together across all sectors.

ABOUT THE AUTHOR

 Jaxon Vale, who specializes in AI-driven tactics that enable people to create scalable enterprises, is an ardent supporter of the nexus between technology and entrepreneurship. Jaxon has been in the vanguard of using artificial intelligence for creative and commercial endeavors, having a background in digital transformation, data science, and machine learning.

Jaxon has offered advice on how to use AI to advance oneself, make money from digital abilities, and expand side projects into successful companies over the years. Jaxon has worked with innumerable budding entrepreneurs, offering them tools, methods, and tips for success in the digital age. He has a natural curiosity and a dedication to helping others achieve.

When not working in the fields of artificial intelligence and business development, Jaxon likes to experiment with new technologies, produce creative digital content, and coach people on how to succeed in the rapidly evolving world of tech-driven opportunities.